CAR

# F is for Friendship
## A Quilt Alphabet

Written by Helen L. Wilbur and Illustrated by Gijsbert van Frankenhuyzen

# A a

Every quilt tells a story. The fabric, the stitching, and design of a quilt tell the story of its making, and sometimes the life of its maker.

A quilt is a bedcover with three layers—a decorative top, a layer of insulation called batting, and a plain back. Quilt stitches go through the layers to keep them in place. Quilting dates back thousands of years. A carpet found in a Mongolian cave is the earliest-known quilted object. The Romans slept on a stuffed sack called a *culcita*, the Latin origin of our word quilt.

Quilting arose from necessity and became a cherished pastime. Although it flourished in North America, quilting knows no boundaries. Its artistry incorporates ideas and traditions from all cultures. The ralli quilts of India and Pakistan, the kente cloths of Africa, the Hmong story cloths all weave their designs and ideas into the tradition of quilting. A beloved quilt gives warmth and comfort and passes on the tradition and spirit of its maker.

A is for Artistry

Pieced from memories, cut with care.
Bound with love, worn, threadbare.
A keepsake, an heirloom—stitched from the heart.
An everyday quilt, a work of art.

What is more snug and comforting than sleeping in your bed under a warm cover? Even people who live in warm climates often sleep under a light blanket. We spend about a third of our lives asleep.

In earlier times people rose with the sun and slept when it got dark. Winters in many parts of the world were cold and light was a precious commodity at night. People slept on mattresses stuffed with straw, husks, wool, or feathers and kept warm under layers of bedcoverings. They often hung rugs or curtains around the beds and windows to keep out drafts and placed heated bricks and warming pans between the covers.

Bedcoverings were made for beauty as well as warmth. A household took pride in offering guests the best bed with a carefully sewn coverlet or quilt used only for special occasions. Covers for beds have many names: blankets, spreads, counterpanes, comforters, comfortables, afghans, puffs, coverlets, quilts.

Whatever you sleep under, have sweet dreams…

B b

## B is for Bedcovers

The night wind drifts across the sill,
bringing with it winter's chill.
My bed's a boat on bright moonbeams,
I'm caught up in a quilt of dreams.

Fabric and clothing play an important part of our lives—for fashion, protection, decoration, and warmth. If you lived before 1800, you probably had only two sets of clothing—one for everyday and another for Sunday. Garments and bedding were so valuable they were often passed down from one generation to the next.

The first high-quality printed cotton originated in Calicut, India, and was called calico. All cloth was woven by hand until a series of inventions in England during the 1700s made machine production possible. England carefully guarded the new manufacturing methods to keep control of all fabric trade. In 1810 an American businessman named Francis Cabot Lowell spied on the British factories and memorized the machinery. He duplicated the power looms in the United States, making printed fabric cheaper and more available.

Fabric selection is one of the most important parts of making a quilt. Cotton remains the most popular choice for quilts. It's soft, durable, and washable. Quilters use all types of fabric as well as personal mementos—like pieces of neckties, dresses, blankets, or uniforms.

## C is for Calico

In my calico dress I cut and piece
calico scraps for Flying Geese.
A calico quilt makes a perfect mat
for the afternoon nap of my calico cat.

# D is for Doll

Miss Hannah takes her tea with milk
and wants a dress of fine green silk.
A quilted petticoat, a shawl—
she's such a prim and pretty doll.

Dolls are one of the most treasured toys of childhood, giving countless hours of companionship and make-believe. A little girl imagines her life and tells her stories through her dolls. Oftentimes, a girl would get her first lessons in sewing by stitching clothes and quilts for her dolls.

In the past, little girls started to learn to sew as early as three years of age. Small quilts with simple designs made easy sewing projects for little hands to hold. By making quilts for their dolls, girls could practice their sewing skills, take pride in their accomplishments, and prepare for their life's work. Being an accomplished seamstress made a young woman a "fine catch" for a young man in marriage and gave her an outlet for earning money when few occupations were available to women outside the home.

# E is for Exhibits

Pigs and cows and chickens—they're
competing at the county fair
with jams and pickles, cakes and pies.
Look! My quilt has won first prize.

Looking, learning, watching, winning—from local church fairs to international quilt shows, quilters love to show and see quilts.

Whether it's for a simple ribbon or thousands of dollars in prize money, quilters have competed since the agricultural county fairs in the nineteenth century. The Sears National Quilt Contest for the 1933 World's Fair theme of "A Century of Progress" drew over 25 thousand entries and sparked interest in national quilt contests. Quilt shows offer prizes in many categories including skill level, featured technique, subject matter, or "best in show." Many shows give prizes to encourage young quilters.

From its humble beginnings at the county fair with the livestock and carnival rides, the quilt has risen to an acknowledged art form hanging in major museums. Quilt artists use traditional forms as well as new materials and techniques to create exciting works of art shown in galleries and collections. Some museums focus exclusively on quilts for historical study and appreciation as well as works of art.

Ee

Since the early quilting bees, quilters gather not just to share work but also to share their lives, their love of quilting, and to help others. Sharing creates lifelong bonds of friendship.

Quilting grew as a popular activity, particularly in rural areas, until interest declined during the 1940s. Women joined the workforce to assist in the war effort and attitudes toward home crafts changed. In the 1970s the U.S. bicentennial and an emphasis on handmade crafts revived quilting as a hobby which continues to grow today.

Quilt clubs and guilds offer an opportunity to meet, attend programs and workshops, exchange skills, and serve the community. Quilters place great importance on public service, producing quilts for disaster relief around the world. With the Internet, quilters now connect across the globe in thousands of quilting blogs, chat groups, and online guilds.

F is for Friendship

We sew each piece and day by day
a pattern starts to find its way.
Stitched together without end,
that's what you are to me, my friend.

Quilting connects generations. Passing down quilting skills, and often a quilt, creates an important family heritage. In 1905 Mary Ambercrombie started a Kansas Sunflower quilt on a cattle ranch in Nebraska that was finished by her great-granddaughter 60 years later.

For early African-American families in slavery, skills were the primary things they had to pass on. African-American women sewed and quilted for plantation owners, taking scraps for the simple clothing and quilts of their own. Two well-known quilters from the nineteenth century were former slaves. One of Harriet Powers's famous pictorial Bible quilts is in the Smithsonian Institution. Elizabeth Keckley bought her freedom with money earned as a seamstress. She sewed for Mary Todd Lincoln and made a quilt from her dress scraps.

An isolated rural community in Alabama called Gee's Bend produced generations of inventive quilters who passed their vivid, abstract styles from mother to daughter. Along with other modern African-American quilters, the Gee's Bend quilters combine traditional styles with bold colors, rhythms, and storylines from their unique heritage.

## G is for Generations

She loved to quilt and then taught me
its comfort, skill, and artistry.
I feel your grandma's strength and grace
each time I see your shining face.

Gg

# H h

## H is for Hands

Each is blessed with two strong hands
to cook and quilt, to work the lands.
Souls together, hearts remain
living simple, living plain.

In 1971 the Whitney Museum of Modern Art in New York City was the first to display a collection of homemade quilts showing quilts as modern art. But the Amish women who made these quilts were from a community where people lived as they did one hundred years ago.

The Amish, like the Mennonites, Hutterites, and similar groups, came to the United States and Canada in the late eighteenth century seeking religious freedom. They settled in farming communities to follow lives devoted to humility, simplicity, family, community, and service. The conservative Old Order Amish and Mennonites, also known as the Plain People, still drive horse-drawn buggies and farm teams, dress in plain clothing, and restrict use of radio, television, electricity, and the Internet.

Quilts from the Amish and Mennonite communities are prized for their strong, simple designs and superb sewing. Amish quilts are usually geometrical patchwork designs made from bright colors that appear to glow from a black or dark background.

Color brightens our world. Artists use color to create a visual impact and convey feeling. Bright colors express energy and excitement while softer colors soothe and calm.

From early times people used dyes to color fabric. Colors were limited to those dyes that could be made from natural sources—plants, animals, and minerals. Dyers used insects or plant roots for red, shellfish for purple, and ochre or saffron for yellow. Indigo, one of the most important natural dyes, came from the leaves of a small shrub and colored fabrics a deep blue. Natural indigo dyes are still used for coloring some blue jeans.

While searching for a cure for malaria in the 1850s, William Henry Perkin accidentally discovered how to make the first synthetic dye. This introduced many new colors for fabrics and quilting. Experts use fabric color and dye to date quilts; quilters use color to create beautiful and eye-catching designs.

The human eye can see millions of colors. Which one is your favorite?

I is for Indigo

Sew me a quilt and if you do
make it white and indigo blue.
I'll save it for best and put it away,
until my wedding day next May.

Quilts mark life's passages: the birth of a baby, marriage, anniversaries, illness, loss. Like journals, quilts tell life stories, not just of an individual but also of families and communities. A young woman used to prepare very early for her role as homemaker and wife. With the help of relatives and friends she sewed and quilted to perfect her skills and to assemble enough bedding and linen for her future household.

Quilts wrap a new baby, honor special occasions, record political events, document family histories. Quilts create memories and honor traditions. They also preserve a moment in time, difficult times that require courage as well as happy times to celebrate. In 1841 a group of women convicts from England sailed on the ship *Rajah* to prison in Australia. Given sewing supplies they created a beautiful quilt on the long voyage. The *Rajah Quilt*, now in the National Gallery of Australia, shows the triumph of hope and imagination under dire conditions.

J j

J is for Journal

For a bride's new bed, a baby's nap,
a special day, an empty lap.
A quilt can serve in countless ways—
a journal of our lives and days.

**K** is for Kapa Moe

Into our quilts we sew the wind,
hibiscus, breadfruit, tamarind.
Our beloved islands' plants and trees,
surrounded by the surging seas.

Hawaiian quilts blend the beauty of island crafts with traditional quilting techniques and materials. Early Hawaiians made *kapa* fabric by pounding the inner bark of a mulberry tree into a paste which was then spread into sheets, dried, and dyed with colorful designs. A *kapa moe* makes a warm, soft, strong, and water-resistant bedcovering.

Contact with western missionaries brought traditional quilting methods and materials to the islands. But the Hawaiians developed a unique method of quilting inspired by their lush landscape and sense of life. Their quilts feature a single design cut from a folded piece of cloth (like cutting a paper snowflake) sewn onto a top of contrasting color. The patterns use native flowers, plants, and everyday objects to recall loved ones, historical events, traditions, and legends. Each quilt has a purpose and many believe it carries the spirit, or *mana*, of the person who made it.

Hawaii's most famous quilt was made by its last queen, Lili`uokalani, in 1895. You can see it today at the Iolani Palace on your next trip to Hawaii.

Kk

# L¹

There are thousands of quilt patterns. Like family recipes and child-rearing advice, over the years women shared patterns with family and friends. As a result, there are no standard names for many patterns, and patterns often have more than one name. The first published quilt pattern appeared in a ladies' magazine in 1835. By the end of the 1800s quilt patterns became regular features in magazines and newspapers. Soon quilt kits with ready-cut pieces made quilting easier and even more popular.

Pattern names come from all aspects of life:

| Theme | Pattern Names |
|---|---|
| Home life: | Pickle Dish, Baskets |
| Farm life: | Hens and Chickens, Hole in the Barn Door |
| The Bible: | Jacob's Ladder, Rose of Sharon |
| Nature: | Bear Paw, Honey Bee |
| Patriotism: | Maple Leaf, Stars and Stripes |

Log Cabin remains one of the most popular patterns. It is formed with strips of cloth, like logs, around a central square, often in red, to represent the hearth.

## L is for Log Cabin

At the little Log Cabin by the tall Pine Tree,
Hens and Chickens spy a Honey Bee.
With Sunbonnet Sue on a Wild Goose Chase,
you can see patterns all over the place.

The morning star holds a special significance for many native tribes. The Lakota Sioux are known for their bright and beautiful eight-pointed star quilts. As their precious buffalo herds dwindled, the Lakota used quilts to replace painted buffalo hide robes. Today quilts are part of Lakota traditions and ceremonies as gifts of honor—for new babies, marriages, graduations, returning veterans, basketball tournaments, and other special events.

A Hopi mother wraps her twenty-day-old baby in a quilt and presents the infant to the rising sun, repeating its name. Relatives and friends gather to celebrate the Naming Ceremony and to welcome a new member into their clan. A Hopi baby may receive many quilts, often featuring traditional designs like kachinas and rattles, or clan symbols.

Native Americans and Canadian First Nations people first learned quilting from European traders and missionaries. They embraced this skill and adapted it to their own customs using tribal legends, colors, and designs. Native quilters draw on their diverse beliefs and legends to introduce new patterns, artistic ideas, and traditions into quilting.

**M** is for Morning Star

Brightest star of the dawning day
        bring us wisdom, guide our way.
Give thanks for all the new day brings,
        for the earth, the sky, all living things.

What weighs 54 tons, got nominated for a Nobel Peace Prize, and is the world's largest community art project? A quilt. To be more specific, the NAMES Project AIDS Memorial Quilt.

A group in San Francisco started the quilt in 1987 to help people understand the magnitude of human loss from the AIDS epidemic. People from all over the country responded immediately, donating panels commemorating friends, loved ones, and well-known individuals who lost their lives to AIDS. The quilt panels contain an amazing array of materials, techniques, and personal mementos, including fur, leather, feathers, T-shirts, boots, jewelry, car keys, stuffed animals, even bowling balls.

A work still in progress, the AIDS Quilt now has over 46 thousand panels commemorating more than 91 thousand people. In a 1996 display in Washington, D. C., the quilt covered the entire National Mall.

N is for the Names Project

It started with one name, that's all,
and grew to fill the National Mall.
Now thousands can participate
to comfort, heal, and educate.

Traveling to the North American West before the transcontinental railroad in 1869 meant an overland journey of three to six months. Settlers loaded covered wagons and set out in early spring to reach their destination before winter set in. People walked most of the way and slept rolled up in blankets or quilts under the stars.

The journey west took a lot of preparation. A wagon needed to carry all the provisions for a family—food, tools, weapons, household items, clothes, and blankets. Women sewed and quilted for months before departure. A Friendship Quilt, with inked signatures and wishes of those left behind, created cherished keepsakes for departing families. Quilts had many uses on the trail besides bedding. They blocked out the wind, rain, and constant dust in the wagons; they also wrapped loved ones who died during the journey. Names of quilt patterns like Rocky Road to Kansas express the hardships of the trails west.

O is for Overland Trails

My cozy quilt is tucked up tight,
I'm ready for the long, cold night.
Underneath the spinning sky,
sing to me a lullaby.

# P is for Patchwork

Sewing the fabric of our lives,
mothers, daughters, sisters, wives.
Patches of sorrow, joy, and strife,
making beauty from the scraps of life.

Patchwork quilts give a great example of making something practical and pleasing out of scraps. In patchwork a quilter cuts many pieces of cloth into geometric shapes and sews them together to form a pattern. Thrifty quilters make string quilts by sewing onto a paper or muslin foundation pieces too small for any other use.

When most family clothing was made at home, leftover fabric and cut-up old clothes became quilt pieces. It was a task of necessity but could also be fun with scraps traded among households. A piece of a treasured wedding or party dress might appear in the quilts of many family members and friends. Old shirts, jeans, uniforms, T-shirts, and blankets, as well as dresses have all been sewn into quilts.

During the times of economic hardship in the 1930s women cut up cotton flour, sugar, and feed sacks for quilts, some with the logo still on them. These quilts in Australia are called *waggas*, said to come from the "Wagga Lily" flour sacks used to make them.

Pp

At a quilting bee friends and neighbors gather to quilt. Before sewing machines a quilt could take months for one person to complete. Many quilters working together could finish one in a day. Back then women quilted on a homemade wooden frame, big enough to seat many participants on all sides, while the hostess prepared a lunch or supper. Younger women learned stitching expertise and everyone shared recipes, advice, stories, gossip, joys, and sorrows. This tradition continues with today's quilters.

Quilting bees also gave women opportunities to discuss political and social events. Susan B. Anthony gave her first speech on equal rights for women at a quilting bee in Cleveland, Ohio. It wasn't until nearly 50 years later that women got the right to vote.

# Q is for Quilting Bee

Come on, sister, don't be shy.
Get ready now to stitch and tie.
Sit by the frame my father built.
By evening we will have a quilt.

Q q

**R** is for Remember Me

The ink may fade, the fabric tear,
the quilt frayed thin with years of wear.
I stitched my name, but let it be—
only this, remember me.

It's rare that an old quilt has the signature of its maker. Made for everyday use, even the "best" quilt was considered a household item not important enough to sign. An old quilt opens a window into the everyday life of those who made it, used it, and cherished it.

Signature quilts, with each block made and signed by a different quilter, became popular in the 1850s with the introduction of indelible ink. Album quilts often included Bible verses or personal messages to the recipient. Signatures inked or stitched on a historical quilt may be the only record of a person's existence. Volunteers for the American and Canadian Red Cross made signature quilts to raise money for wounded soldiers during World War I. People would contribute money to sign the quilt. One of the most famous Red Cross quilts has the signatures of Theodore Roosevelt and Helen Keller.

But, signed or not, sewn into every quilt is the legacy of its maker.

**S** is for Sewing Machine

> Powered by my flying feet,
> making stitches fast and neat.
> My new machine will just amaze,
> it does in hours what once took days.

In the 1850s Isaac Merritt Singer developed a household appliance that changed millions of lives. Working as a machinist in between jobs as a touring actor, Singer figured out how to make the clumsy sewing machines of the day practical for home use. Singer's machine was powered by foot, instead of a hand crank, leaving the sewer's hands free to control the fabric. The machines were expensive and sold poorly at first. At that time women were considered too undependable to operate machines.

Singer's marketing genius removed these doubts. He traveled to stores, theaters, and fairs, having women demonstrate the machines. More importantly, he invented the installment plan which allowed thousands of ordinary households to acquire a sewing machine on credit. For many homes Mr. Singer's machine became the most treasured possession.

The sewing machine dramatically reduced the time required to home sew family clothing and quilts. Today's sewing machines take advantage of new technologies and features which make machine quilting very popular.

When you sew a quilt you can use some of the earliest-known technologies along with the newest. Archeologists have discovered bone needles from the Stone Age used for sewing hides for clothing. The sharp end of the needle cuts through material, pulling thread to bind it together. In fact, quilters call their needles "sharps." Thimbles protect the finger or thumb when a sewer pushes the needle through cloth. Early thimbles have been found in Roman ruins and Chinese excavations from the first and second centuries.

Having the right tools and keeping them in good order are the keys to any endeavor. Hoops, scissors, seam rippers, threads, cutting mats and rulers, rotary cutters, needles, pins, and an iron are all basic needs for the avid quilter. Today's quilter can use computers for designing quilts, scanners for transfer of photographs to fabric, and computer-guided longarm machines for quilting. Yet many quilters still find hand quilting the most satisfying and relaxing way to produce a quilt.

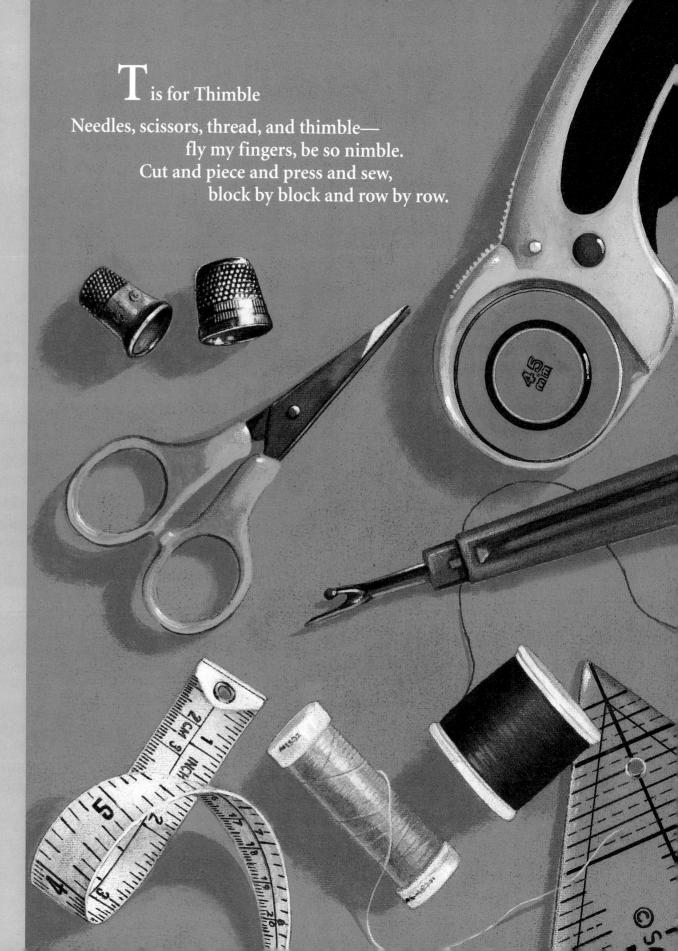

T is for Thimble

Needles, scissors, thread, and thimble—
fly my fingers, be so nimble.
Cut and piece and press and sew,
block by block and row by row.

In 1864, during the U.S. Civil War, a group of schoolchildren made a quilt with an inked message in the center: "Bradford County. For any soldier who loves little children." A soldier in Tennessee received the quilt and wrote to them that he prized the "splendid quilt" and would value it, preserve it, and take it home, if he got to go home.

When the Civil War started in 1861 neither side was ready for war. Soldiers often supplied their own guns, bedding, and uniforms. Women rallied to their cause, picking up their needles to provide husbands, brothers, sons, and neighbors with warm, durable clothing and quilts. Southern women made raffle quilts to raise money for ironclad gunboats. Northern women had a tradition of raising money and awareness with handicraft fairs in support of ending slavery. The U.S. Sanitation Commission distributed nearly 250 thousand homemade quilts to Union soldiers giving them protection and comfort.

Quilters have answered the call in every war ever since, creating timeless gifts of honor and gratitude.

**U** is for Union and Confederacy

This quilt was made with love and care
by our small hands. We give our prayer
it offers comfort, keeps you warm,
until you come home, safe from harm.

V v

V is for Victorian Crazy Quilts

Silks and taffetas, brocades and swirls,
Fancy stitching, ribbons and pearls,
A riot of color confuses my brain …
That's what makes a quilt insane.

What makes a quilt crazy? It follows no set pattern, has vivid colors, rich fabrics, and is decorated with fancy needlework. Crazy quilts became a craze during the Victorian era at the end of the 1800s.

Crazy quilts were made for home decoration rather than warmth; they featured more luxurious fabrics—silk, satin, velvet, and taffeta—and elaborate embroidery. Embroidered animals, flowers, fans, names, quotations, and keepsakes showcased the skill and personality of the quilter.

The Japanese pavilion at the 1876 Centennial Exhibition in Philadelphia exposed new ideas about design to the public. The Exhibition attracted nearly 10 million visitors, twenty percent of the U.S. population at that time, allowing many to see such things as a telephone and steam engine for the first time. Crazy quilting drew on the popularity and fascination with Asian art and culture and unleashed new creativity in home sewing.

**W** is for Womenfolk … menfolk, too!

Supper's eaten, quiltin's done.
Clear the floor, let's have some fun!
Get out the fiddle, goodness knows,
we'll dance until the rooster crows.

Quilting bees and quilting were not just for women. In a time when women mostly worked in the home, a bee gave a woman a showcase for her sewing and cooking skills. Husbands and bachelors often showed up at the end of the day to join in for supper and a dance. Quilting bees made excellent courting opportunities. A young man could show off his flair for dancing and conversation. Everyone could have a good meal and a good time.

Today more and more men participate as quilters, collectors, and scholars. In the 1930s Mr. Albert Small teased his wife about a quilt she and her friends were making. They asked him if he could do any better. So Mr. Small decided to make a quilt with the greatest number of pieces. He made three quilts, the last of which contained more than 123 thousand tiny six-sided pieces. Mr. Small's day job in an Illinois quarry handling dynamite obviously gave him some experience in handling delicate objects with exceptional care.

W
W

# X is for X-Hatch (Cross-hatch)

It's not a song until it's sung.
It's not a swing until it's swung.
It's not a house until it's built.
Without the quilting, it's not a quilt.

Quilters say "It's not a quilt until it's quilted." That seems obvious but what does it really mean? Quilting holds the three quilt layers (top, batting, and backing) together. Quilt layers can be bound together by a small running stitch sewn by hand or machine. A faster and easier method ties the layers at intervals with yard or thread.

Besides holding the quilt together, quilting gives the work texture and shading. The simple grid pattern of the cross-hatch (x-hatch) is the most basic but there are thousands of quilting motifs—lines, diamonds, clamshells, leaves, spirals, ropes, cables, hearts, and feathers to name just a few. The challenge is to match the design of the quilt top with the pattern of the quilting stitches.

Creating an heirloom-quality hand quilt can be very time-consuming. An average quilt will have 50 thousand stitches, large quilts with intricate designs many, many more. Beginning quilters can do five to seven stitches per inch with experts doing twelve or more. No wonder quilting bees became so popular.

# Yy

Shopping wasn't always as easy as going to the mall or ordering over the Internet. If you lived on a farm in colonial times, you bought the things you couldn't make at home from a traveling peddler. Towns and cities had dry goods stores which specialized in fabric sold by the yard and sewing supplies. People living in the country made occasional town visits to stock up on goods, get mail, and visit. The postal service began Rural Free Delivery in 1896, making it possible for people in remote areas to get home mail delivery.

Ladies' magazines offered free quilt patterns, the latest fashions, and domestic advice. People could now shop and get home delivery through catalogs. The Sears Roebuck Company produced a 500-page catalog (popularly called the "Wish Book"), offering everything from fabric to automobiles. Today quilters can shop on the Web or in one of the thousands of specialty quilting shops which offer fabric, sewing supplies, classes, advice, and connections with other quilt enthusiasts.

## Y is for Yard Goods

Stacks of calico and chintz,
wool and cotton, plain and prints.
Pins and patterns, thread and more,
all waiting at the fabric store.

What does math have to do with quilting? Plenty. From crafting the design to figuring out how much fabric to buy, quilters need math. Even simple designs require planning and problem solving. Take the zig zag quilt—you can make it from a series of either rectangles or triangles. (Can you figure out how?) The plainest quilt requires careful measuring to make sure the pieces fit.

A block is the basic unit of most quilt designs. Quilters combine basic geometric shapes—circles, triangles, squares, rectangles, and polygons in a block to make other shapes. Creating space, depth, and regularity from shapes makes use of the basic principles of geometry. Quilters duplicate the blocks in various ways (symmetry) to create patterns. Repeating interlocking shapes (tessellation) makes overall designs like a honeycomb or a brick wall. Color, light, and shade help quilt designs appear to change and move as you look at them.

When you look at a quilt, try to count the number of shapes and see how the quilter has used the combinations to make an amazing design.

Z z

Z is for Zig Zag

Mathematics and geometry
are tools for creativity.
A quilter's crafty calculation
can make a visual sensation.

# Quilt Your Story

### Tell your story, learn about others
Quilts and other family keepsakes can help you discover your family history.

### My story—A quilt and a letter
Gram Short lived by the Merrimack River in a house as small and neat as she was. She was sharp, quick moving, self-contained, and opinionated. Born Lydia Ann Pearson in 1843, Gram married shoemaker Alexander LeRoy Short. Alexander served as a volunteer from Massachusetts during the Civil War. He wrote to her from the battlefield, telling her not to grieve if he did not make it home. The letter began, "Dear Mrs. Short…" When the Merrimack River flooded, Lydia refused to leave her home and

had to be carried out by the local fire department. She was 93. Lydia was my great-great grandmother. Years ago my aunt Myrla rescued Gram's quilt from the trash and carefully saved it along with Grandpa's Civil War letter. Lydia made her quilt over 100 years ago—it reached out to me and inspired this book.

### Your story
You are a part of your family history. Collect your family stories by asking about the keepsakes in your home. What is the oldest item in your home? Where did it come from and why is your family saving it? The things in your room tell a story about you. What would your story be?

—Helen L. Wilbur

# Quilt Quiz

Can you identify some well-known quilt patterns and styles?
Test your knowledge with this quiz.

1. _____ Crazy Quilt

2. _____ Flying Geese

3. _____ Bear Paw

4. _____ Log Cabin

5. _____ Baskets

6. _____ Hawaiian Quilt

7. _____ Lakota Star

8. _____ Zig Zag

**A**

**B**

**C**

**D**

**E**

**F**

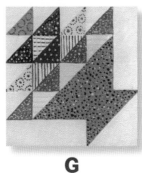

**G**

**H**

*To dear friends Caroline, Pat, Dick, and Mary M.*
*With love and thanks to Aunt Myrla for saving and treasuring Lydia's quilt.*

HELEN

❖

*To the Quilt Queen, you know who you are.*

GIJSBERT

**AUTHOR'S ACKNOWLEDGMENTS:**
The author wishes to thank and acknowledge the following for access to their outstanding collections and library:

International Quilt Study Center & Museum in Lincoln, Nebraska, at www.quiltstudy.org, with particular thanks to Maureen Ose

The New England Quilt Museum in Lowell, Massachusetts, at www.nequiltmuseum.org

Special thanks to quilters Christie Brandau, Karin Peirce, and Lauri Taylor

**ILLUSTRATOR'S ACKNOWLEDGMENTS:**
This book would have been so difficult without the help of expert quilters, friends, and family. The unbelievable kindness of strangers who offered their quilts, their expertise, and especially their "modeling" time was amazing. Huge thanks to Beth Donaldson (collections assistant, Michigan State University Museum) whose expertise was incredible. Special thanks goes to the following individuals: Barb Harris who opened the floodgates to all of my connections; Janice Orlando who arranged meetings with so many of the kids I eventually used as models; Linda Rufenacht (Threads of Tradition Quilt Shop, Sauder Village); Elaine Weijandt and Rhoda King (Sauder Village 34th Annual Quilt Show).

*Models*
Shaye Steitz; William Isabell; Beth Donaldson; Denise and Mary McGinn; Ryan Chapko; Sophie and Emery Miller; Samuel Aylward; Gabbie, Vincent, and Maggie Orlando; Maitri Desai; Denise and Rachel Carethers; Rebecca and Emma Collins; Chihiro Mellon; Victoria Voges; Ben, Rachel and Kelvin Potter; Mary Remenak; Ruth Hodge; Delores Wade; April Brooks; Barb Smith; Jennifer and Pearson Miller; Adam Motley; Charlie Fanta; and Maryanne Boylan

*Quilts & Other Resources*
Beth Donaldson; the Tuesday Sewing Group (the Adrian First United Methodist Church); Emery Miller; Carol Schon, Martha Caterino, Lenora Rathbun, Patricia Clark, Norine Antuck, and Jackie Shulsky (the Wednesday Quilt Club); Maryanne Boylan; Russ Cummins; Mary Remenak; April Brooks; Jennifer Miller; Joan Mason; Julie Tews and Maxine Hartenburg; Lansing Area Patchers Quilt Guild; Michigan State University Quilt Collection; Sauder Village (Archbold, Ohio); Country Stitches (East Lansing, MI)

Sleeping Bear Press®
315 E. Eisenhower Parkway, Suite 200
Ann Arbor, MI 48108
www.sleepingbearpress.com

Sleeping Bear Press is an imprint of Gale, a part of Cengage Learning.

10 9 8 7 6 5 4 3 2 1

Library of Congress Cataloging-in-Publication Data

Wilbur, Helen L., 1948-
F is for friendship : a quilt alphabet / written by Helen L. Wilbur ; illustrated by Gijsbert van Frankenhuyzen.
p. cm.
ISBN 978-1-58536-532-6
1. Patchwork quilts—Juvenile literature. 2. English language—Alphabet—Juvenile literature. 3. Alphabet books. I. Frankenhuyzen, Gijsbert van, ill. II. Title.
TT835.W5324 2011
746.46—dc22                    2010034398

Printed by China Translation & Printing Services Limited, Guangdong Province, China. 1st printing. 11/2010